EXPLORE my world

Koalas

Jill Esbaum

NATIONAL GEOGRAPHIC KiDS

WASHINGTON, D.C.

A koala!

These cuddly creatures are built for life in the trees.

Strong arms and legs? Check. Sharp claws? Yep. Good balance? You bet!

A thick, fuzzy coat keeps a koala cool on warm days and warm on chilly ones. Rain? Not a problem. This coat is waterproof!

The fur on a koala's rounded bottom grows extra thick, so even hard seats feel oh, so comfy.

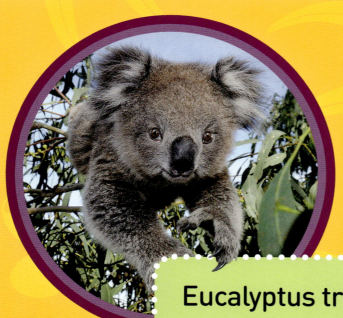

Eucalyptus trees are everything to koalas—a place to hang out, grab some grub, or take a nap.

If a koala is awake and rested, it is eating, grooming, climbing … or ambling along the ground to a different tree.

A koala spends *a lot* of its awake time plucking *a lot* of leathery leaves that need *a lot* of chewing. Most of the water a koala needs comes from the leaves, too.

If a koala gets tired of chewing, it stuffs the gloppy wad of leaves into its cheek to save for later.

Leaves, please!

fruit

bark

What tough food can you chew with your teeth?

Many different kinds of eucalyptus trees grow in koala country. Each tastes different to a koala.

Besides eucalyptus leaves, koalas will nibble the tree's buds, flowers, stems, and bark.

leaves

A koala baby is called a joey. A newborn koala is as small as a bumblebee. Inside its mother's warm pouch a koala changes and grows.

Snuggle

Baby koalas have only one job: drink milk so they grow, grow, grow.

A mother koala hums to her joey. They talk to each other with soft clicks and squeaks.

Pocket protectors!

quokka

wallaby

Koalas are marsupials—animals that carry their babies in body pouches. While in the pouch, a baby grows bigger, stronger, and hairier.

Do you like to be carried?

Where do you curl up to sleep?

opossum

Pouches keep marsupial babies safe until they are big enough to live on their own. Other marsupials include kangaroos, Tasmanian devils, and most opossums.

What do you keep in your pockets?

Can you hop like a kangaroo?

Tasmanian devil

kangaroo

19

G'day!

At about six months old, a brave joey begins leaving the pouch to practice moving around on its own. Reach and pull. Creep and crawl. Careful, junior!

Sooner or later, a joey wants a taste of leaves. Since it hasn't yet learned what its paws are for, it reaches with its mouth. Hold still, leaf!

When a joey feels tired, it slips back into the pouch for a nap.

One day the joey gets too big for the pouch! For the next year or two, the joey sticks close to Mom, learning to be a grown-up.

When the joey is old enough, it goes off to find its own trees. Koalas live alone, and each one needs about 100 trees all to itself.

Rub, rub, rub!

Each koala has its own territory, also called a home range. A male koala rubs its chest against a tree. The smell left behind tells other koalas that the tree is already claimed.

Koalas talk to their neighbors with booming bellows or loud, growly snores.

Sweet dreams

After a busy morning, there's nothing better than snoozing away a sunny afternoon. And snooze they do—for 18 to 20 hours of every day! Good night, koala.

Where Koalas Live

Koalas live in eastern Australia and islands nearby.

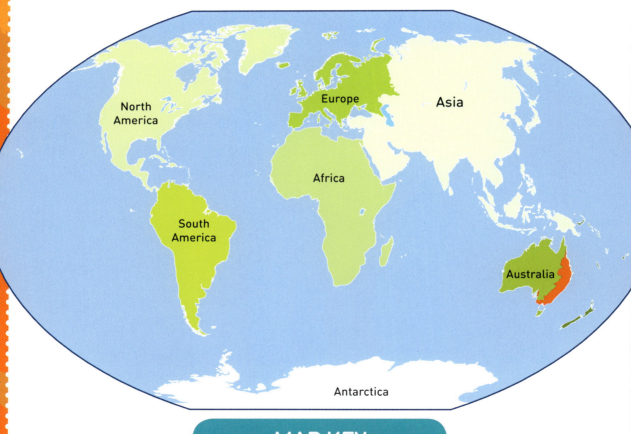

MAP KEY
▪ Where koalas live

Koala Maze

With your finger, show the hungry koala how to get to the yummy eucalyptus leaves.

For Dallas —JE

Copyright © 2015 National Geographic Society
Published by National Geographic Partners, LLC, Washington, D.C. 20036. All rights reserved. Reproduction of the whole or any part of the contents without written permission from the publisher is prohibited.

Since 1888, the National Geographic Society has funded more than 12,000 research, exploration, and preservation projects around the world. The Society receives funds from National Geographic Partners, LLC, funded in part by your purchase. A portion of the proceeds from this book supports this vital work. To learn more, visit natgeo.com/info.

NATIONAL GEOGRAPHIC and Yellow Border Design are trademarks of the National Geographic Society, used under license.

Designed by Amanda Larsen

Trade paperback ISBN: 978-1-4263-1877-1
Reinforced library binding ISBN: 978-1-4263-1878-8

The publisher gratefully acknowledges Dr. Bill Ellis of the University of Queensland's Koala Ecology Group and National Geographic's early education specialist Catherine Hughes for their expert reviews of the book.

PHOTOGRAPHY CREDITS
1, Steven David Miller/naturepl.com; 2–3, Mitsuaki Iwago/Minden Pictures; 4–5, blickwinkel/Alamy; 6, Gérard Lacz/Biosphoto; 7, imageBROKER/Alamy; 8 (UP), Jouan & Rius/naturepl.com; 8 (LO), Frank & Joyce Burek/Animals Animals/Earth Scenes; 9, Mitsuaki Iwago/Minden Pictures; 10, Ardea/Sailer, Steffen & Alexandra/Animals Animals/Earth Scenes; 11, Cyril Ruoso/Biosphoto; 12 (UP), Suzi Eszterhas/Minden Pictures; 12 (CTR LE), Archiwiz/Shutterstock; 12 (CTR RT), Robyn Mackenzie/Shutterstock; 12 (LO), Robyn Mackenzie/Shutterstock; 13 (UP), janaph/Shutterstock; 13 (LO), Miller, Steven David/Animals Animals/Earth Scenes; 14, Suzi Eszterhas/Minden Pictures; 16, Suzi Eszterhas/Minden Pictures; 17, Suzi Eszterhas/Minden Pictures; 18 (UP), Kevin Schafer/Minden Pictures; 18 (CTR), Danita Delimont/Gallo Images/Getty Images; 18 (LO), Cynthia Kidwell/Shutterstock; 19 (LE), Graham Melling/iStockphoto; 19 (RT), idiz/Shutterstock; 20, Suzi Eszterhas/Minden Pictures; 22 (UP), Robyn Mackenzie/Shutterstock; 22 (LO), Suzi Eszterhas/Minden Pictures; 23, Suzi Eszterhas/Minden Pictures; 24, Suzi Eszterhas/Minden Pictures; 26, Lacz, Gérard/Animals Animals/Earth Scenes; 27, blickwinkel/Alamy; 28–29, Cyril Ruoso/Biosphoto; 31 (UP), Gerry Pearce/Alamy; 31 (LO), arka38/Shutterstock; 32, Lacz, Gérard/Animals Animals/Earth Scenes; background (koalas), Rey Kamensky/Shutterstock; background (leaves), Aliaksei/Shutterstock; background (pawprints), elenkorn/Shutterstock

Front cover: (CTR), Gerard Lacz/Kimball Stock; (CTR RT), tubuceo/Shutterstock; (LO RT), Martin Ruegner/Getty Images; back cover: (LO LE), Tim Davis/Getty Images

Collection copyright © 2017 National Geographic Partners, LLC
Collection ISBN (paperback): 978-1-4263-2949-4
Collection ISBN (library edition): 978-1-4263-2950-0

Printed in Hong Kong
17/THK/1

Dolphins

Becky Baines

WASHINGTON, D.C.

Splash!

Diving into blue ocean waters, a bottlenose dolphin gracefully glides under waves and then leaps high in the air!

Dolphins live in family groups. Do you see one, two, three, four? Sometimes there are even more!

Living in a group helps dolphins find food and stay safe. Dolphins must watch out for sharp shark teeth, fishing nets, and boats that buzz by.

In deep ocean waters, groups of dolphins might get together to form a school. A school can have hundreds of dolphins in it! But in shallow water you are more likely to see fewer than 12 dolphins together.

Hello!

Did you know
that dolphins talk?
Instead of words,
they make sounds like
clicks, squawks, and whistles.
Each dolphin has its own
whistle, just like you have your
own name.

A baby dolphin even knows the
sound of its mom's call.

Chow Time!

What's your favorite food?

Dolphins dine on fast fish and slimy squid, crawling crabs, and squirmy shrimp. But it can be hard to see in the dark ocean. How do dolphins find food?

shrimp

fish

squid

12

A dolphin "sees" with sound. As it swims along, the dolphin makes a clicking noise. When the noise hits something in the dolphin's path, the sound bounces back.

That tells the dolphin the size, shape, and speed of its dinner... and right where to find it!

Watch out for those pincers!

crab

What is this dolphin eating for lunch?

Gulp!

Dolphins hunting together swim round and round. They crowd a school of fish into a tight little bunch. Then they take turns swooping in, mouths open for a snack.

Dolphin teeth are shaped like upside-down ice-cream cones. They are great for grabbing!

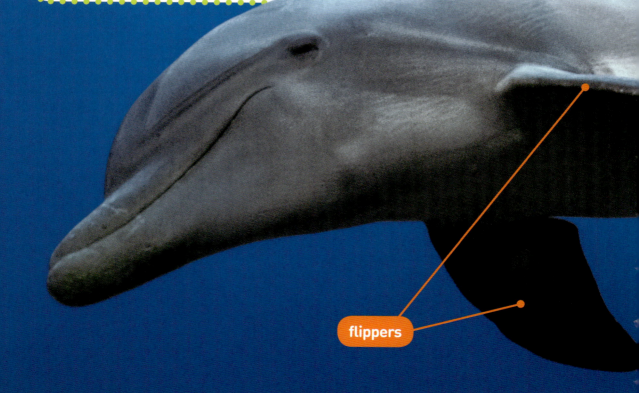

A dolphin's body is made for swimming. They have flippers that help them stop, start, and turn.

flippers

dorsal fin

tail

They have a strong tail that goes up and down, pushing them forward, fast. They have a big dorsal fin that keeps them swimming straight.

Marine Mammals

Dolphins are mammals—just like you!

Mammals are warm-blooded. A dolphin's body stays at a comfy 97°F.

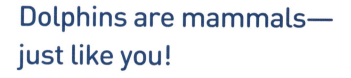

Your normal body temperature is a warm 98.6°F.

Mammals have backbones. A dolphin's backbone bends so it can move its powerful tail.

Mammals have hair. Dolphin babies have hair on their noses!

Baby mammals drink their mom's milk. Dolphin babies need lots of milk to grow big and strong.

Do you have a tail?

What did you eat when you were a baby?

Can you touch your backbone?

Oh baby!

A baby dolphin, called a calf, is born just under the surface of the water. It is about the same size as a six-year-old boy or girl.

An adult dolphin takes a newborn calf up to the surface for a big breath of air. The calf pops out of the water and breathes through a hole in the top of its head.

The calf starts to swim right after it is born.

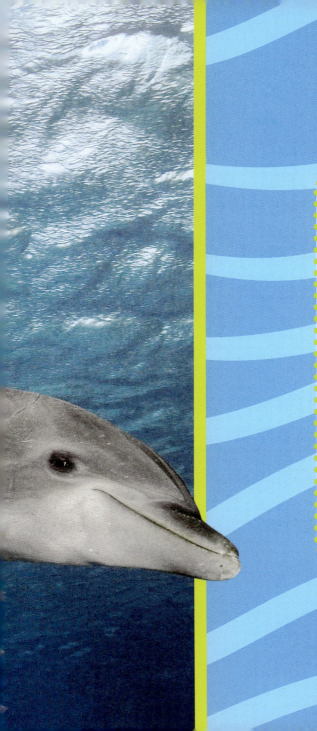

Grown-up dolphins have a layer of fat called blubber that keeps them warm, but calves don't. They keep warm by keeping up! Lots of mammals move around to stay warm.

In days, calves start to talk with the rest of the group.

In about six months, calves begin to eat fish.

For about three years, a calf stays with its mother. When a dolphin is around six years old, it is all grown up.

Playtime!

Being a dolphin isn't all hard work. They enjoy fun and games!

Dolphins ride waves. *Yippee!*
They blow bubbles. *Boing!*
They leap high in the air.
Whee!

Night, night!

When the day is done, you might find dolphins playing games in the moonlight, feasting on fish and squid.

Or they might rest for a little while. Good night, dolphin!

Different Dolphins

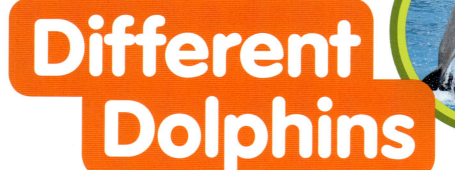
bottlenose dolphin

orca

There are 43 different species, or kinds, of dolphins. The bottlenose dolphin is the most famous. These mammals live in oceans around the world. Some even live in rivers and lakes. If you ever go dolphin-watching, here are a few species you might meet.

For Ellie Boo

Copyright © 2016 National Geographic Society

Published by National Geographic Partners, LLC, Washington, D.C. 20036. All rights reserved. Reproduction of the whole or any part of the contents without written permission from the publisher is prohibited.

The publisher gratefully acknowledges Bruno Diaz Lopez, Chief Biologist and Director, Bottlenose Dolphin Research Institute, Pontevedra, Spain, for his expert review of the book.

Designed by Amanda Larsen

PHOTOGRAPHY CREDITS

1 (CTR), Wyland/SeaPics.com; 2-3 (CTR), Roland Seitre/Minden Pictures/Corbis; 4-5 (CTR), Brandon Cole; 6 (CTR), Minden Pictures/Getty Images; 7 (BACKGROUND), TSHOOTER/Shutterstock; 7 (UP RT), Doug Perrine/SeaPics.com; 7 (LO LE), Evlakhov/Shutterstock; 8-9 (CTR), Petra Wegner/Alamy; 10 (CTR), Universal Images Group/Getty Images; 11 (UP RT), Augusto Stanzani/ARDEA; 12 (UP RT), Jeff Rotman/Getty Images; 12 (LO LE), schankz/Shutterstock; 12 (LO RT), seksan wangjaisuk/Shutterstock; 12 (CTR LE), Weerachai Khamfu/Shutterstock; 13 (UP RT), chungking/Shutterstock; 13 (LO RT), Dickie Duckett/Minden Pictures; 14 (CTR), Doug Perrine/Alamy; 15 (CTR), Universal Images Group/Getty Images; 16-17 (CTR), Doug Perrine/SeaPics.com; 18 (LO LE), Alexey Tkachenko/Getty Images; 18 (UP RT), Francois Gohier/VWPics/Alamy; 18 (LO RT), Denniro/Shutterstock; 19 (LO CTR), Barry B. Brown/wildhorizons.com; 19 (UP RT), DmitriMaruta/Shutterstock; 19 (CTR RT), Hurst Photo/Shutterstock; 20 (BACKGROUND), yyang/Shutterstock; 20 (UP LE), Augusto Satanzini/ARDEA; 21 (CTR), Tim Davis/Corbis; 22-23 (CTR LE), Universal Images Group/Getty Images; 24 (UP LE), Natalia Pryanishnikova/Alamy; 24 (LO RT), Nature/UIG/Getty Images; 25 (CTR), Universal Images Group/Getty Images; 26 (CTR), Masa Ushioda/SeaPics.com; 27 (UP LE), Stone/Getty Images; 27 (LO RT), Fco. Javier Gutiérrez/fotostock/Spain S.L./Corbis; 28-29 (CTR), Panoramic Images/Getty Images; 30 (LO LE), Martin Ruegner/Getty Images; 30 (UP RT), Natali Glado/Shutterstock; 31 (CTR LE), Kevin Schafer/Minden Pictures/Corbis; 31 (UP LE), Todd Pusser/SeaPics.com; 31 (LO LE), Andy Murch/SeaPics.com; 31 (CTR RT), Jody Watt/Design Pics/Corbis; 31 (LO RT), Matt9122/Shutterstock; 32 (LO LE), Augusto Stanzini/ARDEA

Library of Congress Cataloging-in-Publication Data

Baines, Rebecca, author.
 Dolphins / by Becky Baines.
   pages cm. — (Explore my world)
 Audience: Ages 3-7
  ISBN 978-1-4263-2318-8 (pbk. : alk. paper) — ISBN 978-1-4263-2319-5 (library binding : alk. paper)
  1. Dolphins—Juvenile literature. I. National Geographic Society (U.S.) II. Title. III. Series: Explore my world.
 QL737.C432B355 2016
 599.53—dc23
                         2015027842

EXPLORE my world

Penguins

Jill Esbaum

NATIONAL GEOGRAPHIC KiDS

WASHINGTON, D.C.

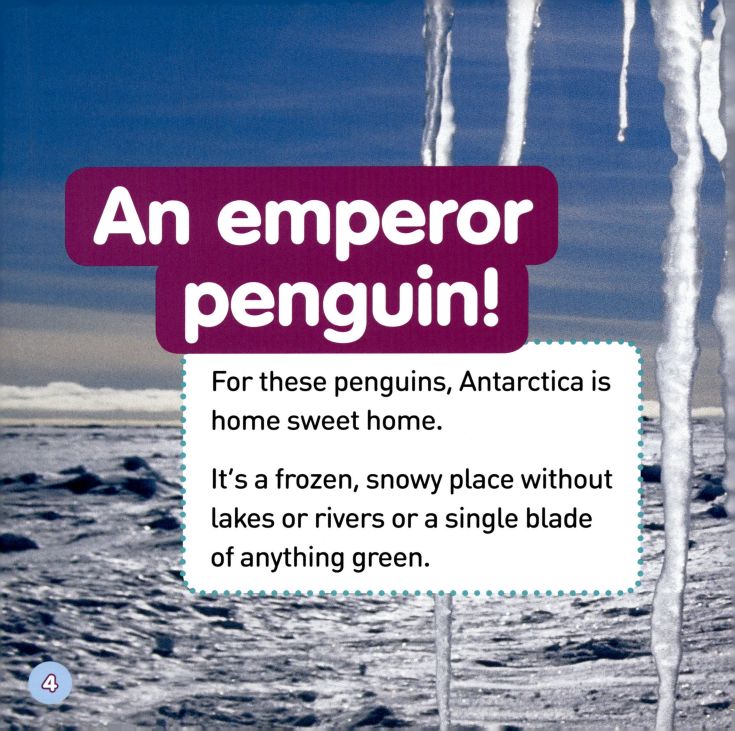

An emperor penguin!

For these penguins, Antarctica is home sweet home.

It's a frozen, snowy place without lakes or rivers or a single blade of anything green.

Waddle!

This tall-as-a-first-grader bird doesn't mind that the temperatures are below zero—*waaaay* below zero.

Their bodies are perfect for a refrigerated life.

A baby penguin would not survive long in this frozen world by itself. Luckily, emperor parents know how to protect their little one.

After Mom lays an egg, she rolls it from her webbed feet onto Dad's. Oops, careful!

When the egg is safely atop Dad's feet—whew!—he lowers a special feathered pouch to keep it cozy.

Mom leaves right away. She needs to find food, and for that, she must travel to the sea.

She will walk many miles before reaching water. Her leathery feet march across the snow. Her sharp claws grip icy spots.

When she finds the sea, Mom will feast for weeks.

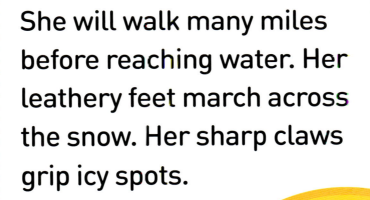

Brrr. Why Antarctica?

Can you waddle like a penguin?

How can penguins live in Antarctica?

Leathery, webbed feet are great for standing on ice and swimming!

How do you keep your feet warm?

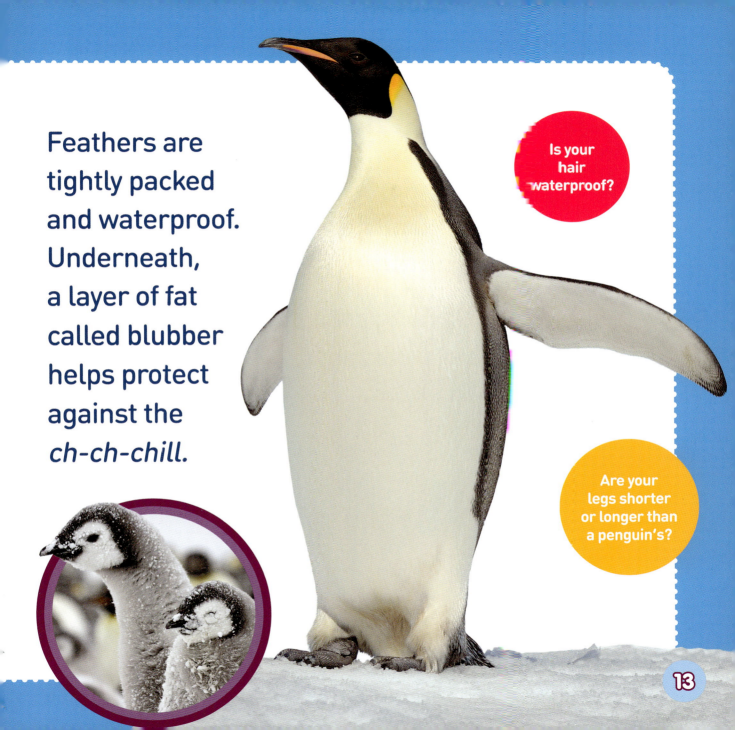

Feathers are tightly packed and waterproof. Underneath, a layer of fat called blubber helps protect against the *ch-ch-chill.*

Is your hair waterproof?

Are your legs shorter or longer than a penguin's?

Shiver!

Bone-chilling cold. Icy winds. Blizzards.

The penguin dad stands through it all, keeping the egg safe and warm. He does not get a break for two long months—not even to eat.

To keep from freezing, all the father penguins in a group, or colony, huddle close together. They take turns shuffling into the toasty middle, then out again.

Mom penguin returns to the colony in July or August. She and Dad call back and forth until they find each other.

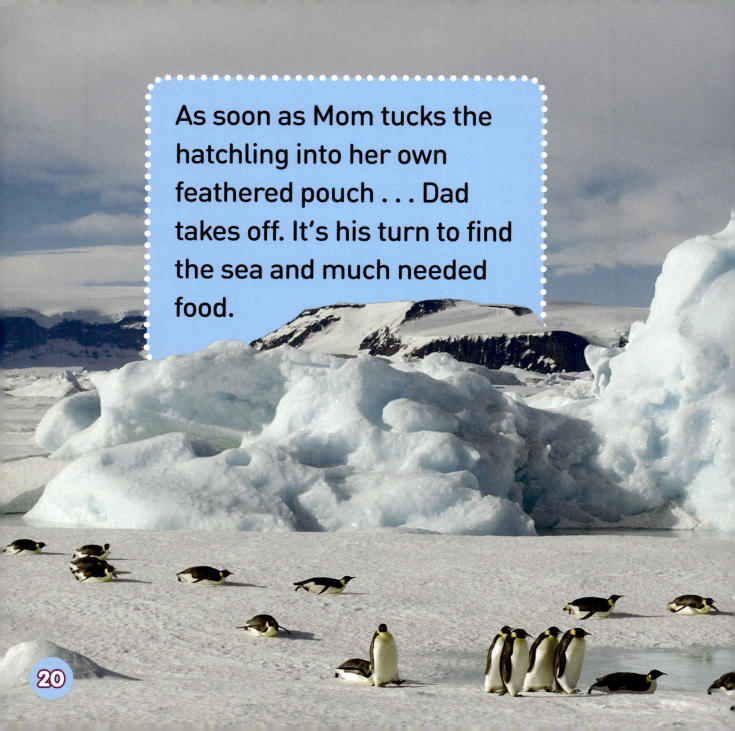

As soon as Mom tucks the hatchling into her own feathered pouch . . . Dad takes off. It's his turn to find the sea and much needed food.

Like Mom, he waddle-walks over miles of ice and snow. He sometimes flops forward to toboggan, pushing with his feet and flippers.

What's for Lunch?

Would penguins eat carrots?

What do emperor penguins eat?

Penguins eat food found only in the sea, like Antarctic silverfish, hooked squid, and Antarctic krill.

Do you eat fish?

From their colony, penguins might have to walk 50 miles (80 km) to find open (unfrozen) water.

They dive deeper than any other bird—to 1,850 feet (565 m). And they're able to stay underwater for 15 to 20 minutes without taking a breath!

Can you swim underwater?

Should you walk on ice quickly or slowly?

Glurp!

Mom penguin's belly is still full of seafood. She brings bits up into her mouth to feed her chick.

The fuzzy chick grows bigger. Braver. It pops out to take a look at the wide, white neighborhood and toddles over the snow to meet new friends!

Summer arrives in December, and ice near the colony breaks up. An adult penguin chicksits while Mom goes off to fish.

Dive, penguin!

At last the penguin is big enough to try swimming and fishing on its own. *Sploosh!*

Penguin Map

There are 17 different types of penguins! Most of them live in Earth's Southern Hemisphere along the coast. Follow the key below to see where on Earth some of these penguins live.

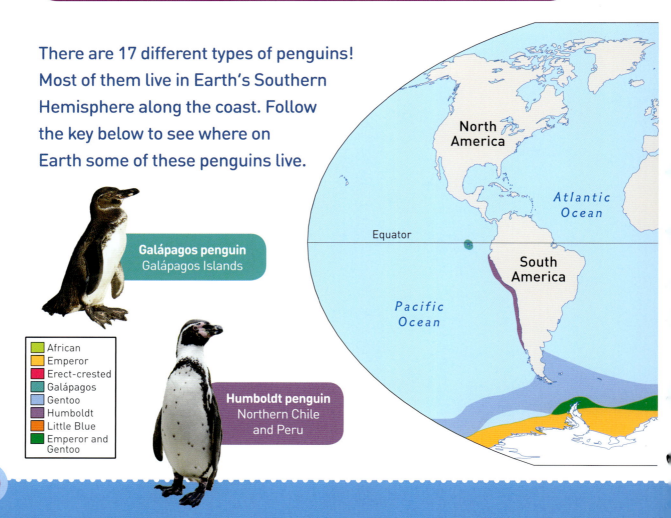

Galápagos penguin
Galápagos Islands

Humboldt penguin
Northern Chile and Peru

Key:
- African
- Emperor
- Erect-crested
- Galápagos
- Gentoo
- Humboldt
- Little Blue
- Emperor and Gentoo

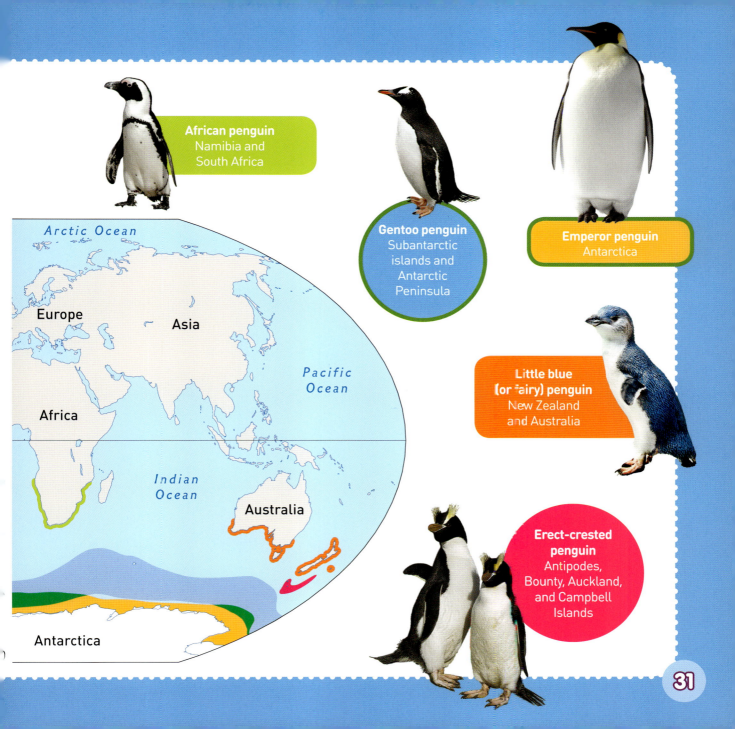

For Grant and Olivia
—JE

Copyright © 2014 National Geographic Society
Published by National Geographic Partners, LLC, Washington, D.C. 20036. All rights reserved. Reproduction of the whole or any part of the contents without written permission from the publisher is prohibited.

Designed by Amanda Larsen

Trade paperback ISBN: 978-1-4263-1701-9
Reinforced library binding ISBN: 978-1-4263-1702-6

The publisher gratefully acknowledges Dr. Gerald Kooyman of Scripps Institution of Oceanography and early education expert Catherine Hughes for their expert reviews of the book.

ILLUSTRATIONS CREDITS
1, David Tipling/naturepl.com; 2–3, Tui De Roy/Minden Pictures; 4–5, W.Lynch/Arcticphoto.com; 6, Cordier Sylvain/hemis.fr/Getty Images; 7 (background), ivivankeulen/Shutterstock; 8, Fred Olivier/naturepl.com; 8 (background), Denis Barbulat/Shutterstock; 9, Pete Oxford/naturepl.com; 10, Paul Nicklen/National Geographic Creative; 11, Bob Smith/National Geographic Creative; 11 (background), ntnt/Shutterstock; 12 (UP), Paul Nicklen/National Geographic Creative; 12 (LO), Paul Nicklen/National Geographic Creative; 13 (LE), David Rootes/Arcticphoto.com; 13 (RT), blickwinkel/Alamy; 14, Frans Lanting/Mint Images/Getty Images; 15, Fritz Poelking/Picture Press RM/Getty Images; 16–17, Doug Allan/naturepl.com; 18 (UP), Jeff Wilson/naturepl.com; 18 (LO), Paul Souders/WorldFoto; 19, Doug Allen/naturepl.com; 20, Paul Souders/WorldFoto; 21, Armin Rose/Shutterstock; 22 (UP), Nattika/Shutterstock; 22 (CTR), panda3800/Shutterstock; 22 (LOLE), George F. Mobley/National Geographic Creative; 22 (LORT), Paul Nicklen/National Geographic Creative; 23 (UP), Frans Lanting/National Geographic Creative; 23 (LO), Paul Nicklen/National Geographic Creative; 24, Paul Nicklen/National Geographic Creative; 25 (UP), Paul Souders/WorldFoto; 25 (LO), J.-L. Klein & M.-L. Hubert/Biosphoto/Minden Pictures; 26, Sue Flood/naturepl.com; 27, Paul Nicklen/National Geographic Creative; 28–29, Paul Nicklen/National Geographic Creative; 30 (UP), gynane/iStockphoto; 30 (CTR), GoodOlga/iStockphoto; 30 (LO), Jeff Mauritzen/NGS; 31 (UP), Coldimages/iStockphoto; 31 (UP LE), George F. Mobley/National Geographic Creative; 31 (CTR), Stephen Meese/iStockphoto; 31 (LO), Tui De Roy/Minden Pictures; 32, Konrad Wothe/Minden Pictures